P9-DOB-374

GUIDE TO
JAPAN

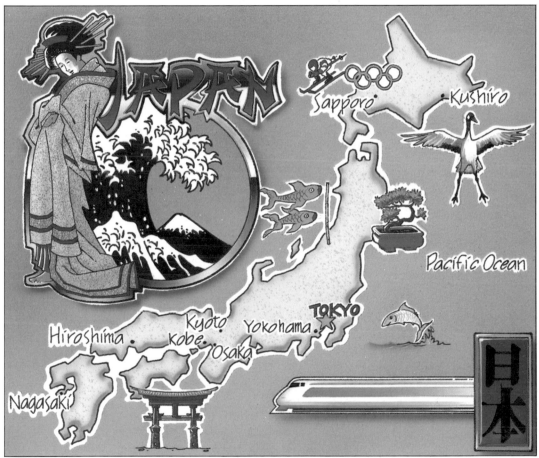

Sapporo · ·Kushiro

Pacific Ocean

TOKYO

Kyoto· Yokohama·
Hiroshima · Kobe· · ·
·Osaka

Nagasaki

日本

MICHAEL MARCH

Highlights for Children

LIBRARY
FRANKLIN PIERCE COLLEGE
RINDGE, NH 03461

CONTENTS

Japan at a Glance 4

The Sunrise Islands 6

The Eastern Capital 8

Upriver in Tokyo 10

Shoguns and Emperors 12

The Quiet Volcano 14

Historic Cities 16

An Industrial Giant 18

Sacred Places 20

The Western Frontier 22

Bullfights and Pilgrims 24

Going North 26

Japan Facts and Figures 28

History and Language 31

Index and Acknowledgments 32

On the cover:

Beyond a typical Japanese pagoda is a great view of Mt. Fuji, Japan's highest mountain. It is a dormant volcano.

CORR
DS
806
.M373
1995

64t 4/03

Published by Highlights for Children

© 1995 Highlights for Children, Inc.
P. O. Box 18201
Columbus, Ohio 43218-0201

All rights reserved. No part of this book may be reproduced or transmitted in any form or by any means, electronic or mechanical, including photocopying, recording, or by any information storage and retrieval system, without permission in writing from the publisher.

10 9

ISBN 0-87534-911-0

NORTH AMERICA

Tropic of Cancer

Equator

SOUTH AMERICA

Tropic of Capricorn

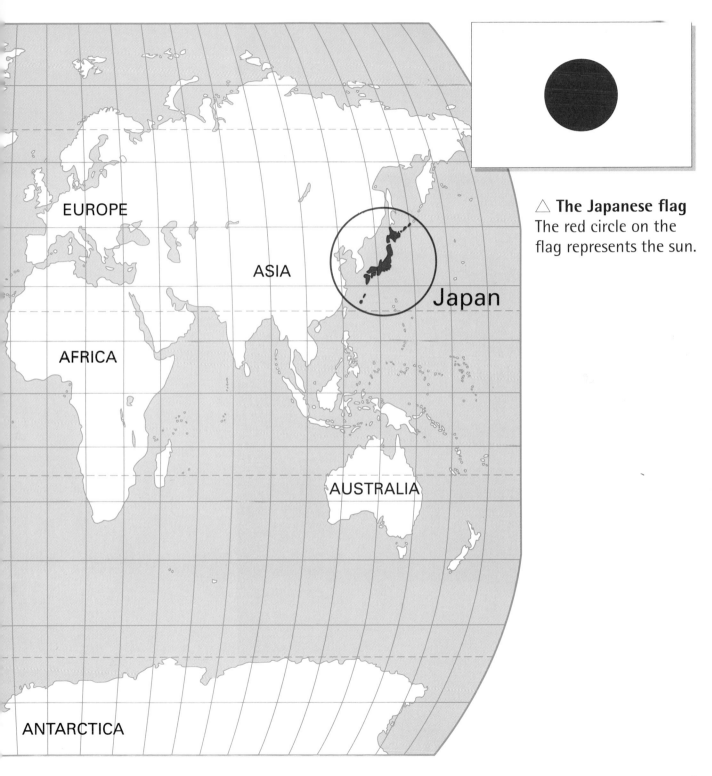

EUROPE

ASIA

AFRICA

Japan

AUSTRALIA

ANTARCTICA

△ **The Japanese flag**
The red circle on the
flag represents the sun.

JAPAN AT A GLANCE

Area 145,800 square miles (377,700 square kilometers), made up of some 4,000 islands

Population 124,336,000

Capital Tokyo, population of city and surroundings is more than 12,000,000

Other big cities Yokohama (population 3,250,000), Osaka (2,495,000), Nagoya (2,095,000)

Highest mountain Mount Fuji, 12,388 feet (3,776 meters)

Longest river Shinano-gawa, 228 miles (367 kilometers)

Largest lake Lake Biwa, 260 square miles (674 square kilometers)

Official language Japanese

▽ **A selection of Japanese postage stamps**
They show examples of Japanese art, past and present, and of Japan's rich birdlife. The country has over 400 species of birds.

◁ **Japanese bank notes**
Japanese currency is the yen (¥). There are bills of ¥1,000, ¥5,000, and ¥10,000. The ¥1,000 bill shows the writer Soseki Natsume on one side. The other side features the crane, symbol of long life.

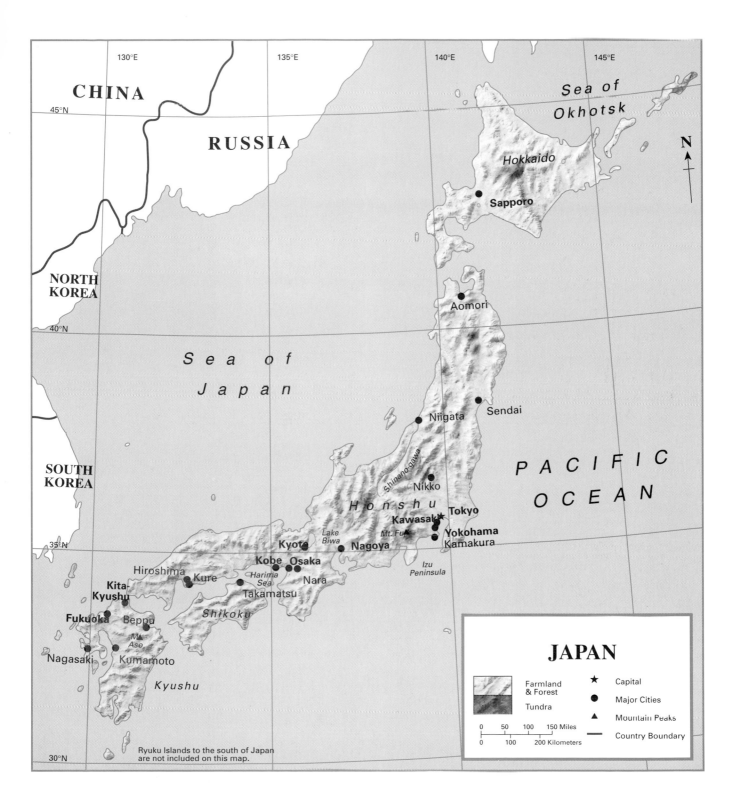

CHINA

RUSSIA

Sea of
Okhotsk

N

130°E   135°E   140°E   145°E

45°N

Hokkaido

● Sapporo

NORTH
KOREA

40°N

Sea of
Japan

● Aomori

SOUTH
KOREA

PACIFIC
OCEAN

Niigata   Sendai

Shinano-gawa

35°N

Nikko ●

H o n s h u

Kyoto   *Lake*   **Nagoya**   **Kawasaki** ★ **Tokyo**
                  Biwa   Mt. Fuji ▲   **Yokohama**
                                                        Kamakura

Hiroshima   *Harima*   Nara   *Izu*
              Kure   *Sea*   *Peninsula*

Kobe ● **Osaka**

Kita-
Kyushu   Takamatsu

Fukuoka ●   Beppu   *Shikoku*

              ▲
              Aso

Nagasaki   Kumamoto

Kyushu

30°N

Ryuku Islands to the south of Japan
are not included on this map.

JAPAN

Farmland & Forest	★ Capital
Tundra	● Major Cities
	▲ Mountain Peaks
	— Country Boundary

0   50   100   150 Miles

0   100   200 Kilometers

THE SUNRISE ISLANDS

Japan is a chain of some 4,000 islands off the east coast of mainland Asia. The Japanese call their country *Nippon*, meaning "land of the rising sun." According to legend, it was put on Earth as a gift of the gods.

The four main islands are Honshu, Kyushu, Shikoku, and Hokkaido. Most of Japan's 124 million people live in the lowlands of Honshu, the biggest island.

Mountains cover three-quarters of the country. There are forests on most mountain slopes, and swift-flowing rivers. Japan currently has 67 active volcanoes and is shaken by a major earthquake every five years or so. Typhoons in late summer are another major hazard. On the southern islands, summers are hot and humid. To the north near Hokkaido, winters are so cold that the sea freezes over.

About half of the farmland is planted with rice, the country's most important crop. Rice is the staple food of the Japanese people and has been for centuries. Most of it is grown on small family farms.

Japan is a modern country, whose cars and televisions are famous throughout the world. It is also a land of age-old traditions and customs. The language is based on written Chinese but is very different from it. It is also like no other language. People from the big cities take part in festivals dating back hundreds of years, and they follow two of the oldest religions, Shinto and Buddhism.

As you travel around the country on some of the world's fastest express trains, the *shinkansen*, you will see examples of the old and the new all around you. Welcome to Japan.

△ **A religious festival procession** Many such events are held throughout the year. They are part of the Japanese way of life.

◁ **Rice fields under Mount Aso, Kyushu** Rice seeds are planted during the rainy season in flooded fields called paddies.

▷**Three little children wearing yukata, or summer kimonos** The *kimono* is a traditional Japanese robe that is wrapped around the body and tied behind with a sash.

THE EASTERN CAPITAL

At the heart of Japan is its capital, Tokyo. This huge city of 12 million people lies on the south side of the Kanto plain, on the island of Honshu. It is the center of government, business, industry, broadcasting, and the press.

Tokyo began as a small fishing village called Edo. In the 15th century Edo became a city. Later it was a stronghold of the medieval warlord Ieyasu Tokugawa. In 1868, the emperor Meiji moved the capital from Kyoto to Edo. The emperor also changed its name to Tokyo, which means "eastern capital."

▽ **A kabuki performance** In these colorful, costumed musical dramas, the women's parts are traditionally played by men.

8

Much of Tokyo was destroyed by an earthquake in 1923, and again by bombing in World War II. Since then, the city has been transformed into a bustling modern metropolis. It is full of people on the move, crowded streets, factories, shops, and office blocks.

Getting around Tokyo is easy for foreign visitors. If you use the subway, avoid the crowded rush hours. And should you lose your way, look for the police boxes, called *kobans*, where you can get help.

Although there are few old buildings left to visit in Tokyo, the city has many other attractions. Ginza is the best-known shopping district. Akihabara displays the latest in electronic goods, like computers and camcorders, which have made Japan famous. There are many thousands of restaurants in the city. They offer a wide selection of Japanese and foreign foods. If you want a taste of old Japan, you can visit a *kabuki* theater. Here, actors perform a 300-year-old type of drama.

◁ **Shinjuku at night**
By day, Shinjuku is one of Tokyo's busiest districts. Some 2 million subway commuters pass through it twice a day. At night, it is an entertainment center.

▷**Tokyo Stock Exchange**
From here shares of stock worth billions of Yen are bought and sold every day. Tokyo is one of the world's biggest financial centers.

UPRIVER IN TOKYO

The Japanese love to eat fish. Tokyo's fishmarket is the biggest in the world. It stands on land near the mouth of the Sumida River. There, early in the morning, you will find the wholesalers who supply shops and restaurants with fish. They shout their bids for the best of the day's catch.

From the jetty nearby, you can board the "river bus." This is a double-decker, glassed-in ferry that can carry more than 500 passengers. It runs to and from Asakusa, a district once famous for its bars, evening entertainment, and kabuki theater.

△ **A Sumo wrestling contest** The aim is to push an opponent out of the ring, or to make him lose his balance.

◁ **The Tokyo "river bus"** The ferry passes under 11 bridges as it goes up the Sumida River on its way to Asakusa. It runs every half hour.

▷**Tsukiji fishmarket** From here, fish are taken to other parts of the country. Trains run to the market to collect the fish, so they will stay as fresh as possible.

On the river trip, you will notice the green roof of the Kokugikan. This is the headquarters of *Sumo* wrestling. Sumo is the Japanese national sport and belongs to a tradition 2,000 years old. The Sumo tournaments held in Tokyo three times a year attract large audiences. Before a tournament, the huge Sumo wrestlers may be seen praying at Asakusa's Senso-ji, the oldest Buddhist temple in Tokyo. Kabuki players also go to the temple. They pay their respects to Kannon, the goddess of mercy, before the new theater season opens.

There is a Japanese saying, "Never say magnificent till you've seen Nikko." This ancient city is famous for its temples and shrines. It is about two hours north of Asakusa by train. The main attraction of Nikko is the Toshogu Shrine, which has elaborately carved statues of animals and gods. Many are covered in gold. It was built in honor of Ieyasu Tokugawa by his grandson. Every year, in May, people in historical costumes carry portable shrines through the streets of Nikko. The festival honors Ieyasu and other medieval rulers.

SHOGUNS AND EMPERORS

South of Tokyo and beyond Yokohama lies the historic city of Kamakura. It is surrounded on three sides by hills. On the fourth side is the sea. In 1192, the great warlord Yoritomo Minamoto took control of the country from a stronghold here. For nearly 150 years, Japan was governed by the warlords of Kamakura.

▽ **A man in samurai costume** The samurai were expert swordsmen and archers. They were also skilled in unarmed combat, from which sports such as judo have developed.

Yoritomo was buried here, and you can visit his modest tomb. He was Japan's first shogun, or military ruler. The country's emperor lived in the capital, Kyoto, but true power was in the hands of the shogun.

The warlords of Kamakura were *samurai*. This class of warriors lived and died by a strict code of honor. The code was based on Zen Buddhism, a religion that came from China. The gigantic bronze statue of the Great Buddha in Kamakura is one the finest examples of Buddhist art. It once stood in a wooden temple, but this was washed away by a tidal wave in 1495.

To the north of Kamakura is Yokohama. Today, it is a modern, thriving port and the second largest city in Japan. It first became important when nearly 700 years of shogun rule were brought to an end.

From the 17th century, the shoguns had forbidden all contact with foreigners. Then, in 1853, U.S. commodore Matthew Perry arrived with his fleet. He forced Japan to open up to the outside world. The emperor was restored as the most important person in the country once more. A district of Yokohama was set aside for the foreign traders. You can still see some of their houses today. As trade with the rest of world increased, this small fishing village expanded into a busy port.

A major landmark on the skyline of modern Yokohama is Marine Tower. At 348 feet (106 meters) high, it is the tallest lighthouse in the world and offers a fine view of the city.

▽ **Yokohama shipyard** Shipbuilding and oil refining are two of Yokohama's main industries.

◁**Kamakura's Great Buddha** Cast in bronze in 1252, it stands 44 feet (13.3 meters) high.

THE QUIET VOLCANO

Rising 12,388 feet (3,776 meters) from near sea level, Mount Fuji is Japan's highest peak. It is also a volcano. But for nearly 300 years now, the mountain has been quiet. It last erupted in 1707, dropping fine ash as far away as Tokyo.

The Japanese call their mountain *Fuji-san*. It is a national symbol, and the people hold it sacred. Every summer, thousands make the long climb to the top to visit a shrine near the peak. Others go to enjoy the view.

Shrines belong to the ancient Shinto religion, which is not found outside Japan. Shinto is based on the belief that there are spirits in natural things such as mountains, trees, and rivers. There are shrines all over Japan and in many people's homes. Religion is not taught in schools, but you will often come across children in uniform visiting an ancient shrine. Their teacher brings them here as part of a history lesson.

▽ **Schoolchildren practicing Japanese writing** Using brush strokes to form the characters is called calligraphy.

▽ Mount Fuji in the winter
The beauty of the volcano's near-perfect cone shape has inspired artists and poets through the ages.

▽ Inside a Japanese home
The traditional low table and sliding wall contrast with the modern furniture and "high-tech" equipment in the room.

To climb the sacred mountain, you need a sturdy pair of boots. You also need protection from the sun by day or cold at night. The hard journey is worth the effort. Watching the sun rise from the summit on a clear day is an unforgettable experience.

To the south of Mount Fuji is the Izu Peninsula. This is a region with over 2,000 hot springs, and a favorite resort. Here, you can stay in a *ryokan*, a Japanese inn. This is supplied with spring water for bathing. The rooms have sliding paper walls. Inside a ryokan, you sit on cushions on a floor of straw matting called *tatami*. Before entering, you remove your shoes and put on slippers, just as you would do if invited to a Japanese person's home. Meals are served at a low table in your room by a maid in a kimono. The low table is called a *kotatsu*. In winter, quilts are placed over the table and a heater underneath to keep the sitters' legs warm. The bathroom is communal, or shared. Bathing follows the Japanese custom. First you wash yourself. Then you relax in a big tub of hot water along with other guests.

HISTORIC CITIES

For more than a thousand years, the capital of Japan was not Tokyo, but Kyoto. You can reach the old capital from the new on the shinkansen. This trip on the "bullet train" takes less than three hours.

Kyoto has some of the finest old buildings in Japan, including more than 2,000 Buddhist temples and Shinto shrines. Kyoto is also known for its traditional handicrafts. Among these are wooden and ceramic dolls, and baskets and vases made from bamboo. Folding fans were first made in Kyoto, too.

In the city center stands Nijo Castle. This was built in 1603 by Ieyasu Tokugawa, the shogun, to show that his power rivaled the power of the emperor. Here, too, in the castle in 1868, the Emperor Meiji signed the documents that finally abolished the shoguns. The castle has many secret rooms, which you can visit. Its floors creak to warn of approaching footsteps.

The Ryoan-ji Temple, in western Kyoto, is famous for its rock garden, which consists of just 15 rocks. They are set in groups on a bed of coarse gravel raked into a beautiful pattern. The garden was created by a Zen Buddhist monk in the 16th century. It is greatly admired for its simple design.

Even older than Kyoto is the city of Nara, to the south. Here, you will find, among its many historic buildings, the Horyu-ji Temple. This is the oldest temple in all Japan. From here Buddhism gradually spread to cities, towns, and villages across the whole country.

Nara was established as Japan's capital in 710. During this period, culture, religion, and the arts were all under Chinese influence. Rice cultivation, silk weaving, and writing were among the skills that came to Japan from China down through the centuries. So too were dyeing cloth and making lacquerware and porcelain.

▽ **The Keihan electric railway in Kyoto**
The service runs between Kyoto and Osaka.

◁ **Ripening rice** The first storehouses for rice grain gave the basic design for the Shinto shrine.

▽ **Kinkaku-ji (Golden Pavilion), Kyoto** The temple dates from the late 14th century. It was rebuilt in 1955 after a bad fire.

AN INDUSTRIAL GIANT

The growth of the port city of Osaka is an example of Japan's success as a trading nation in recent times. A quarter of all Japanese goods come from here. As an industrial and business center, it is second only to Tokyo.

Osaka sits on the delta of the Yodo River and its many branches. The city has a history of trading and business that goes back some 2,000 years. In the 16th century, the shogun Hideyoshi Toyotomi built Osaka Castle to show off his strength. It was the largest castle in the land. The original castle no longer exists, but you can visit a copy of it built on the same site.

▽ **A Japanese car assembly plant** The Japanese were the first to use robots in their car factories. Here, a group of robots are building the body of a car.

18

◁ **Osaka Castle** The present castle, built in concrete in 1931, is a copy of the original one that dates from 1586.

∨ **An electronics factory** Here, components are being tested. Electronic goods are Japan's biggest export.

Here, too, you will find Japan's newest international airport. It rises out of Osaka Bay on land reclaimed from the sea.

Industry and trade with the rest of the world have made Osaka and Japan rich. Japan now leads the world in car production, motorcycle manufacturing, and shipbuilding. But the most spectacular success has been in making and selling high-technology goods —— from cameras to computers and compact disc players.

Japan needs its foreign trade to pay for imports of the fuel and raw materials that it lacks. Most of the country's electricity is generated from Middle Eastern oil. Foreign iron ore and coal supply its steelmaking plants. Japan also imports more than a quarter of its food.

Every working day at Japan's major seaports, you can see cargoes being unloaded, or loaded for export. One of the busiest is Kobe, which is a 30-minute train ride away from Osaka. Kobe is also famous for its beef. Some Kobe cattle are pampered animals that are massaged and given beer as part of their diet.

SACRED PLACES

To the Japanese, the small island of Miyajima is sacred. It is also one of Japan's most scenic spots and a popular resort. Here, you can enjoy a deer park and wooded hillsides. And, from the top of Mount Misen, there is a fine view of Hiroshima in the distance. But most visitors come to see the shrine that "floats" on the water.

By ferry from Hiroshima, it takes just over 20 minutes to reach the Miyajima. The Itsukushima Jinja Shrine is its religious center. It was first built in the 6th century and has been rebuilt many times since then. The building stands offshore on wooden stilts. At high tide, it does indeed appear to float. In front of it, is a *torii* – the open gateway that you find at most Shinto shrines. It rises 53 feet (16 meters) out of the water. Near the exit to the shrine is the Treasure House. It contains precious gifts to the gods to thank them for past victories in battles on the Inland Sea.

▽ **Itsukushima Shrine**
The shrine and its torii, in the center, are reflected in the water. Visitors are captivated by the beauty of the scene.

◁ **Hiroshima's Peace Memorial Park**
Children bring paper cranes — symbols of
long life — to the children's monument.

The city of Hiroshima, on western Honshu, has other, more recent sacred places and memorials. August 6 is remembered throughout the world as Hiroshima Day. On that date in 1945, a U.S. Air Force plane dropped an atomic bomb that destroyed much of the city. Soon after, World War II ended.

Today, Hiroshima is a modern industrial city, completely rebuilt, but very aware of its past. In its center is Peace Memorial Park, dedicated to the many victims of the atomic blast. There, a flame burns, which will be put out only when all weapons of mass destruction are destroyed.

▽ **Visitors feeding the deer in the park on Miyajima Island**

THE WESTERN FRONTIER

Kyushu is the closest of the main islands to the Asian continent. The shinkansen from Honshu runs as far as Fukuoka, Kyushu's largest city. Here at Hakata Bay, you will find white, sandy beaches and the remains of a once huge stone wall. The wall was built in the 13th century to keep out Mongol invaders. They were finally defeated when a typhoon destroyed their fleet.

The coast road goes south to Nagasaki. It winds around scenic bays and past mountains, forests, and pretty villages. Inland, the small town of Arita is famous for its porcelain. This tradition goes back to the first Korean potters who settled there about 400 years ago.

At about that time, the Portuguese, Dutch, and Spanish began trading with Japan through the port of Nagasaki. When the shogun closed Japan's borders, Nagasaki was the only point of contact with foreigners for more than 200 years. During World War II, it became the second city to be struck by an atomic bomb. However, you can still find many old buildings within the rebuilt, modern city as well as a Peace Memorial Park.

Across the Ariake Sea from Nagasaki is the city of Kumamoto. This has one of Japan's most beautiful landscape gardens and a famous teahouse. The first tea seeds to arrive in Japan were brought to Kyushu from China over 800 years ago.

Sitting in the middle of Kyushu is Mount Aso. This volcano still smoulders after 30 million years. You can approach the crater's edge and watch the smoke rising from deep within the Earth. Kyushu's volcanic soil has made it popular as a health resort. At the southern tip of the island, Ibusuki is famous for its hot sand baths. Beppu, on the northeast coast, has more than 3,000 hot springs.

▷ **Nagasaki and its harbor, seen from above** Today Nagasaki is a thriving seaport whose main activities are shipbuilding and fishing.

▽ **Traditional tea ceremony** In silence, the hostess makes green tea, pours some into a bowl, stirs it with a bamboo whisk, and gently hands the bowl to the guests.

▽ **Ibusuki's natural sand baths** Attendants dig a hole and bury guests up to the neck in the hot sand. It is said to be relaxing. The heat comes from a nearby hot spring.

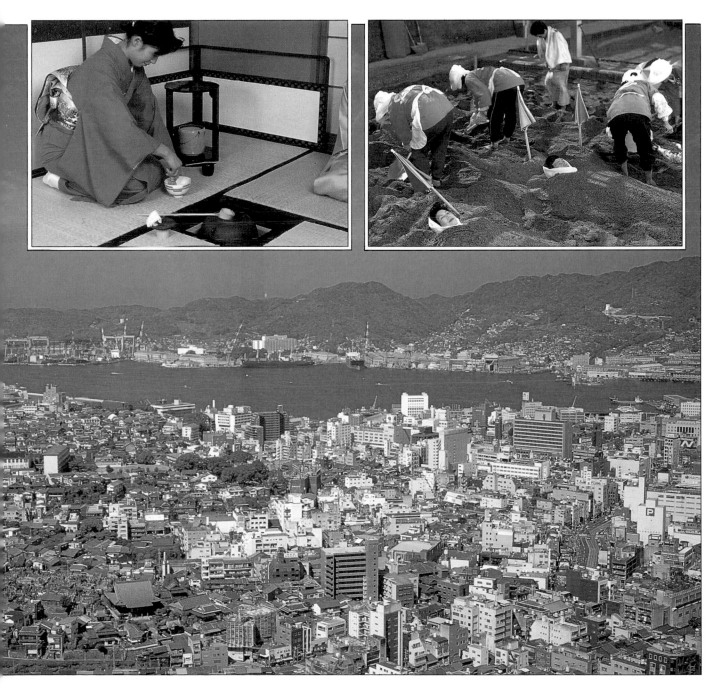

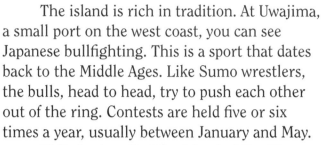

BULLFIGHTS AND PILGRIMS

Crossing the Bungo Channel from Kyushu to Shikoku by ferry takes several hours. Shikoku is the smallest of the four main islands. It is largely unspoiled. Except for the northern coast, it has little industrial development. More of the people here work on farms than in factories. Steep mountains divide the island into north and south and offer spectacular, rugged scenery. Down in the valleys, some villages look as if they are untouched by the passing of time.

The island is rich in tradition. At Uwajima, a small port on the west coast, you can see Japanese bullfighting. This is a sport that dates back to the Middle Ages. Like Sumo wrestlers, the bulls, head to head, try to push each other out of the ring. Contests are held five or six times a year, usually between January and May.

Shikoku is called the island of the 88 temples. As you travel around, you may come across Japanese pilgrims dressed in white.

◁ **A vegetable seller on Shikoku** The island's mild climate is good for growing fruit and vegetables. Tea is also grown here.

▽ **A Shikoku dairy farmer** Japanese people today consume more meat and milk than they used to.

The pilgrims plan to visit all the temples. These people are followers of the Buddhist saint, Kukai, who was born on the island in 774.

The finest of the temples is the Ishite-ji Temple at Matsuyama, a two-hour train ride from Uwajima. It was founded in the 8th century. Japanese people occasionally come here to pray for a cure for their illnesses or injuries. Near the temple is Dogo Onsen, a hot spring resort believed to be 2,000 years old.

The railroad runs along the coast to Takamatsu in the northeast, where you will find Ritsurin Park. This lovely old landscaped garden, with its many hills and ponds, covers an area of over 185 acres (75 hectares). It took almost 100 years to complete.

The garden has a museum of folk art, where local handicrafts are displayed. It also has an exhibition hall, where goods are sold. Here, you can buy masks and locally-made kites.

▷**A selection of Japanese dishes** Fish is a major part of the Japanese diet. It is often eaten raw. *Sashimi* is finely cut slices of raw fish with herbs, raw vegetables, and seaweed.

GOING NORTH

The huge Seto Bridge carries traffic over the Inland Sea between the islands of Shikoku and Honshu. From Okayama, on the Honshu side, you can take a train ride over mountains to the west coast of the island. From here, the railroad to the north hugs the shore, passing forests, farms, and more mountains. Northern Honshu, called Tohoku, is popular as a summer resort. But the region is cold in winter. The best rice and the purest water in Japan are said to come from Tohoku.

From Honshu, you can reach Hokkaido, the northernmost of the main islands, through the world's longest undersea tunnel. Hokkaido is the last home of the Ainu. It is believed that these people once lived farther south, but were driven out by the Yamato, the people who make up most of the population of present-day Japan. There are now very few Ainu left.

▽ **Snow Festival** In the town of Yokote in Tohoku, children build snow houses and set up altars inside them.

◁ **A fishing boat unloads its catch on Hokkaido** The ports of Hokkaido handle one-fifth of all the fish that Japanese fishermen take from the seas.

Hokkaido is rich in natural beauty. There are mountains, lakes, hot springs, volcanic craters, and rugged coastlines. Bears roam free in its forests. Towns are few and farmland plentiful. Most of the country's larger farms are on Hokkaido. Fishing, coalmining, and logging are important to the island, too.

Here you will find no monuments to Japan's distant past. The chief city, Sapporo, was built only some 120 years ago. It was designed by an American. Today it is a popular skiing resort and has hosted the Winter Olympic Games.

Winters are cold on Hokkaido. The first snow falls in November. Sapporo's annual Snow Festival, held in February, draws many thousands of tourists. They come to see the huge ice sculptures. Although Hokkaido is very different from the rest of Japan, it is no less fascinating to visit.

▽ **An Ainu elder** The Ainu were the first people of Japan. They probably came from Siberia long ago.

Japan Facts and Figures

People

The Yamato Japanese make up most of the present-day population. They are a mixture of east Asian and Pacific races. About 600,000 Koreans from the Asian mainland have settled in Japan. The Ainu, who live on Hokkaido, are a separate people. They are believed to have come from Siberia. Now there are about 10,000 Ainu left.

Trade and Industry

Japan has very few mineral resources of its own. Some oil and coal are produced on Honshu and Hokkaido, but most has to be imported. Metal ores, timber, natural gas, and foods are among Japan's other major imports.

To pay for these imports, Japan exports a variety of goods. It produces more steel than any other country. It is also the number one motor vehicle manufacturer. Japan builds 13 million cars and trucks and 5 million motorcycles every year. It is the world's leading shipbuilding nation. However, its greatest export is electrical and electronic goods such as televisions and computers.

A cheerleader dances at a Japanese sports festival.

Farming

Only about one-eighth of the land of Japan is suitable for farming. The most important crop is rice. Rice is grown in flooded paddy fields or on terraced hillsides. After rice, the main crops are potatoes, onions, and mandarin oranges. The raising of beef and dairy cattle for meat and milk is also an important industry.

Fishing

Japan is the world's leading fishing nation with an annual catch of more than 10 million tons. Many types of fish are eaten. These include plaice, cod, tuna, and octopus, as well as shellfish.

Food

Japanese people eat mostly rice, fish, eggs, and vegetables. The main meal is eaten in the evening. People eat from small bowls, using chopsticks. Japanese usually drink water or *sake*, a type of wine made from rice. Green tea is served at the end of the meal.

Some well-known Japanese dishes include:
sushi : small cakes of cold cooked rice wrapped in seaweed often with raw fish.
sukiyaki: thin slices of beef fried with leeks, mushrooms, and Chinese leaves, or other vegetables. It is seasoned with sake and soy sauce, and dipped in raw egg before eating.
tempura: shrimp and slices of fish, with vegetables. They are battered in flour, deep fried, and dipped in soy sauce with horseradish.

Schools

All children must go to school for at least nine years. Many children of preschool age also attend nursery schools.

From the ages of 6 to 12, children go to primary school. They spend the next three years at junior high school. The majority of children complete three more years at senior high school. After that, many go on to one of the 900 universities in the country.

Schoolchildren in Japan work very hard. Classes are held from Monday to Friday, morning and after-noon, and on most Saturday mornings.

The Media

NHK, the Japanese Broadcasting Corporation, broadcasts radio and television programs in several languages, including English. There are also private broadcasting corporations, including some that relay TV pro-grams by satellite or cable.

Japan has 125 different daily newspapers, which together sell more than 70 million copies. There are also thousands of maga-zines and comics to choose from.

Close-up of a face on a traditional, hand-painted kite

Drama

Traditional Japanese theater is still performed today. The oldest is *Noh*, in which the actors, all of whom are men, are masked. In *bunraku*, puppets, two-thirds life size, are worked by three pup-peteers dressed in black. *Kabuki* is a costumed musical drama in which all the parts are usually played by men wearing make-up.

Art

Traditional musical forms, like the *gagaku*, the 11th-century music of the imperial court, are still practiced. Among young people, Japanese popular music and folk music have a large following.

Other traditional arts include *bonsai*, the art of growing potted miniature trees, and *ikebana*, the art of flower arrangement. Also popular is *origami*, the art of paper folding.

Religion

Japan has two major religions, Shinto and Buddhism. Most people follow both. Shinto is a purely Japanese religion. There are many gods and goddesses in Shinto, with more than 80,000 public shrines built to honor them. Buddhism is based on the belief that all creatures are born, die, and are born again. Zen Buddhism, which the samurai followed, puts importance on self-control and meditation.

Christianity was introduced to Japan from Europe in the 16th century. Today, there are about 130,000 Japanese Christians.

JAPAN FACTS AND FIGURES

The Shichi-Go-San festival for children aged 7, 5, and 3 — the Shinto lucky numbers

Sports

Japan's national sport is *Sumo* wrestling. The wrestlers, who follow a special diet, weigh up to 350 lbs (159 kilograms). Contests take place in a circle, or ring. The winner is the contestant who forces the opponent out of the ring or makes him touch the floor with any part of his body apart from his soles.

Judo is a sport that developed from the unarmed combat techniques of the samurai. In *karate*, participants strike with their hands and feet. *Kendo* is based on sword-fighting, but contestants use swords made of bamboo rather than steel.

Baseball, introduced by the Americans, is very popular in Japan. It is often played in schools. The Japanese also enjoy table tennis, golf, soccer, volleyball, tennis, skiing, and fishing.

Festivals and Holidays

There are many festivals held throughout the year in Japan. Most of them are based on religion. In the next column are listed a few of the national holidays:

January 1 **Shogatsu** Women put on their best kimonos, and the doorways of houses are decorated with pine shoots and bamboo.

May 5 **Children's Day** Little boys tie decorated cloth or plastic fish to poles outside the house.

August 13–16 **Obon Festival** A Buddhist festival in honor of one's ancestors

October 10 **Sports Day** To commemorate the Olympic Games held in Tokyo in 1964

December 23 The **Emperor's birthday**

Plants

With over 1,000 species of trees and shrubs, Japan has a very rich plantlife. The types range from tropical mangrove forests on southern Kyushu to alpine plants and creeping pine on northern Hokkaido. Bamboo forests are found in southern Japan.

The Japanese admire cherry trees for their beautiful flowers. In the spring, many parks are filled with the sweet smell of cherry blossoms.

Animals

Japan's wildlife is equally rich and varied. The red-faced macaque lives farther north than any monkey. In winter, it digs in the snow for its food. Some Japanese fishermen train cormorants to catch fish from the sea for the macaques. The giant salamander, found in mountain streams of Honshu and Kyushu, grows up to 5 feet (1.5 meters) in length. The giant spider crab is found in few areas off the coast. It has a shell 12 inches (30 centimeters) across, and legs that span 13 feet (4 meters). Poisonous sea snakes live in the warmer waters around the islands of Japan.

HISTORY

People first settled in Japan about 20,000 years ago. By the 5th century AD, a state had grown up in the Yamoto region of central Japan, and it traded with China and Korea.

In 710, the emperor set up his capital at Nara, but in 794 it was moved to Kyoto. This was the official capital till 1868.

From the 12th century, the samurai, a class of warriors, began to take control of the country. Their leader was the shogun. He was the real ruler of the country, though the emperor remained on the throne.

The first European traders and Christian missionaries arrived in the 16th century. In 1600, Ieyasu Tokugawa became shogun after defeating his rivals. His family remained in power until 1868.

Fearing the influence of Europe, in 1637 Japan shut itself off from the rest of the world for more than 200 years. Then, in 1853, the United States forced the shogun to renew contact with the West and begin trading again. Emperor Meiji deposed the shogun, and moved the capital to Tokyo.

During World War II (1939-1945), Japan bombed the U.S. naval base at Pearl Harbor, Hawaii. Near the end of the war, U.S. planes dropped atomic bombs on Hiroshima and Nagasaki, to force Japan's surrender. Over the past 30 years, Japan has grown into one of the world's great industrial and trading nations.

LANGUAGE

For many years, Japanese existed only as a spoken language. In about 400 AD, China introduced its own writing system to Japan. This system uses characters, or symbols, and not letters of an alphabet. The Japanese used the Chinese characters to develop their own written language. But in many ways, the two languages are very different. Today, about 2,000 of the original 40,000 Chinese characters are used for writing Japanese.

Useful words and phrases

English	Japanese
Zero	ze-ro
One	i-chi
Two	ni
Three	san
Four	shi, yon
Five	go
Six	ro-ku
Seven	na-na, schi-chi
Eight	ha-chi
Nine	kyu
Ten	ju
Sunday	ni-chi-yo-bi
Monday	ge-tsu-yo-bi

Useful words and phrases

English	Japanese
Tuesday	ka-yo-bi
Wednesday	su-i-yo-bi
Thursday	mo-ku-yo-bi
Friday	kin-yo-bi
Saturday	do-yo-bi
Good morning	oha-yo go-zai-ma-su
Hello, good day	kon-ni-chi-wa
Good evening	kom-ban-wa
Good night	o-ya-su-mi na-sai
Goodbye	sa-yo-na-ra
Please	o-ne-gai shi-ma-su
Thank you	a-ri-ga-to
How do you do?	ha-ji-me-mashi-te

INDEX

Ainu 26, 27, 28
Akihabara 9
animals 30
Ariake Sea 22
Arita 22
art 29 see also kabuki
Asakusa 10, 11
Aso, Mount 7, 22

Beppu 22
Biwa, Lake 4
Buddhism 7, 11, 12, 16, 17, 24, 25, 29, 30
bullet train see shinkansen
bullfighting 24
Bungo Channel 24

cars 18, 19, 28
cherry trees 30

Dogo Onsen 25
drama 29

earthquakes 6, 9
Edo 8
electric and electronic goods 19, 28

farming 28
festivals and holidays 7, 26, 27, 30
fish and fishing 10, 25, 27, 28
flag 3
food 19, 25, 28
Fuji, Mount 4, 14, 15
Fukuoka 22

Ginza 9

Hakata Bay 22
Hiroshima 20, 21
Hokkaido 6, 7, 26, 27, 28
Honshu 6, 8, 21, 28
Horyu-ji Temple 16

Ibusuki 22, 23
industry 18, 19, 28
Ishite-ji Temple 25
Itsukushima Jinja Shrine 20
Izu Peninsula 15

kabuki 8, 9, 10, 11, 29
Kamakura 12, 13
Kannon 11
Kanto plain 8
karate 30
kendo 30
kimono 7, 15
Kinaku-ji Temple 17
kobans 9
Kobe 19
Kokugikan 11
Koreans 28
Kukai 25
Kumamoto 22
Kyoto 8, 16, 17, 31
Kyushu 6, 7, 22

language 7, 31

Marine Tower 12
Matsuyama 25
media, the 29
Meiji 8, 31

Minamoto, Yoritomo 12
Misen, Mount 20
Miyajima Island 20, 21
Mongols 22
motorcycles 28

Nagasaki 22
Nagoya 4
Nara 16, 31
Natsume, Soseki 4
Nijo Castle 16
Nikko 11

Osaka 4, 16, 18, 19

people and population 4, 6, 8, 28
Perry, Matthew 12
plants 30

religion 7, 14, 29 see also Buddhism, Shinto
rice 7, 16, 26, 28
Ritsurin Park 25
river bus 10
Ryoan-ji Temple 16
ryokan 15

sake 28
samurai 12, 31
Sapporo 27
schools 29
Seto Bridge 26
Shikoku 6, 24
Shinano-gawa River 4
Shinjuku 9
shinkansen 16, 22

Shinto 7, 14, 16, 17, 20
shoguns 12, 31
Snow Festival 26, 27
sports 30
springs, water 22, 23, 25
Stock Exchange, Tokyo 9
Sumida River 10
Sumo wrestling 10, 11

Takamatsu 25
tatami 15
tea 22, 23, 24, 28
Tohoku 26
Tokugawa, Ieyasu 8, 11, 16, 31
Tokyo 4, 8, 9, 10, 11
Toshogu Shrine 11
Toyotomi, Hideyoshi 18
trade and industry 28, 31
trains 7, 16
Tsukiji fishmarket 10
typhoons 6

Uwajima 24

volcanoes 6, 14, 15, 22

warlords 12

Yamato 26, 28
Yodo River 18
Yokohama 4, 12, 13

Zen Buddhism 12, 16, 29

Book produced for Highlights for Children, Inc. by Bender RIchardson White
Editor: Lionel Bender
Designer and make-up: Malcolm Smythe
Art Editor: Ben White
Editorial Assistant: Madeleine Samuel
Picture Researcher: Annabel Ossel
Production: Kim Richardson

Maps produced by Oxford Cartographers, England
Banknotes from Thomas Cook Currency Services
Stamps from Stanley Gibbons

Managing Editor, Highlights New Products: Margie Hayes Richmond
Editorial Consultant: Andrew Gutelle
Guide to Japan was produced with the assistance of the Japan National Tourist Organization, London
Japanese Consultant: Tamo Hozumi

Picture Credits: EU = Eye Ubiquitous, JNTO = Japan National Tourist Organization, Z = Zefa
t = top, b = bottom, l = left, r = right
Cover: Z/J. F. Raga. Pages: 6b Z/Orion Press. 6-7 Z/Orion Press. 7. Z/Orion Press. 8b, 8-9 Z. 9 EU. 10b JNTO. 10t Z. 11 JNTO. 12 EU. 13bZ. 13t EU/P. Thompson. 14Z/Dr. G. Haasch. 14-15 Z/Orion Press. 15 Z. 16t, 16b EU/Frank Leather. 17 Z/J Schorken. 18-19, 19 Z. 20 Z/Orion Press. 21t EU/Trisha Rafferty. 21b EU/Paul Seheult. 22-23 Z/Orion Press. 23tl JNTO. 23tr EU/J. Holmes. 24l EU/ Paul Seheult. 24r EU/ J. Holmes. 25, 26 JNTO. 26-27 EU/ J. Holmes. 27 Z/ Tony L. Tona. 28 Z/G. Haasch. 29 EU/Ben Spencer. 30 EU/Frank Leather
Illustration on page 1 by: Tom Powers